Acknowledgments
My thanks to my wife Brooke,
Joan Flynn for her help, to
Gregor Larsen for photography
and to Peggy Larsen for design.

Front Cover Quilt

John Flynn, *King's X*, 96" x 108"
Six-strip border is 18" wide with
12" repeat. Center of 6" blocks is
Barbara Johannah's *Governor's
Palace Maze* design.

Additional copies of this
book may be ordered from
Flynn Quilt Frame Company
1000 Shiloh Overpass Road
Billings, Montana 59106

ISBN-0-9627889-1-0

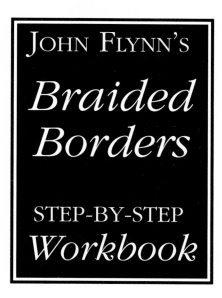

JOHN FLYNN'S
Braided Borders
STEP-BY-STEP
Workbook

*The book at the end of the rainbow!
You'll find endless possibilities
for John Flynn's Braided Border.
Color photographs and coloring
pages help you design your project.
Step-by-step instructions make
constructing this exciting
border easy.*

CONTENTS

Judy Harris. *Braided Mini Dots.*
24" x 27" A four-strip border
4 1/2" wide with a 3" repeat.
The 9 patch center is floated
within the border.

Barb Olson. *Painted Desert.* 48" x 60"
Three-strip border is 6" wide with a 4" repeat.
Strip-pieced center, Nancy Brenan Daniel's
"Mesa Grande" pattern, floats in border.

Braided Borders

Brooke Flynn. *Wandering Fans.* 40 1/2" x 49 1/2"
Four-strip shaded Braided Border of custom dyed fabrics.
Border is 6 3/4" wide with a 4 1/2" repeat. Fits center of 9" blocks.

Introduction

I developed my rainbow Braided Border for a quilt top I've yet to finish. The braided rainbow was too bold for my "Spirals" quilt, so I constructed a bold new center to go with the rainbow border. "King's X" is the result.

I do not know if this border style has been done before — I have not seen it. This workbook is my answer to the many requests I've had for the pattern for "King's X." The emphasis is on planning and constructing the border, but instructions for completing the center are included (page 24).

Before I began teaching my Braided Border class, I was not aware of the infinite possibilities of this pattern. I learn new and different looks each time I teach the class — and each of these new looks spawns a hundred or so ideas. The braided rainbow on "King's X" is as bright as any I have seen. The same color combination in pastels could be used for a more subdued look. The shaded braided border on "Brooke's Fans," page 3 , is my favorite so far. The shaded panels make it easier for my eye to follow the braid, and I am more comfortable with it. Any combination of fabrics can be used to make the braid. You can even make each strand of the braid from a different set of fabrics, as on Joan's "Apple Basket" quilt on page 7. On some of the examples illustrated, the border really is the quilt.

This pattern also has wonderful possibilities as an edging on clothing, pillowcases, table linens.

The actual construction of the Braided Border is very simple.
All of the seams are straight with no set-in corners, and very few points
to match. The three most important things to remember are ACCURACY,
ACCURACY and, of course, ACCURACY. Accuracy when you cut the strips.
Accuracy when you sew. And, accuracy when you cut the panels.

The border is pieced from three basic pieces —

SQUARE PANELS   INSIDE TRIANGLES   OUTSIDE TRIANGLES

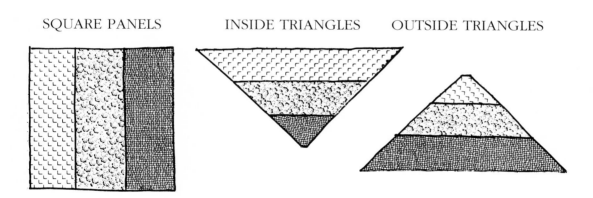

All illustrations in the workbook of the three-strip border —
planning charts and coloring sheets are included for 2,3,4,5 and 6-strip
borders. Examples of most can be found in the quilts pictured.

I suggest that you read through the entire workbook and get
a general idea of the steps involved before you begin your project.

Peggy Larsen. *Ride 'em Cowboy.* 60" x 60"
Six-strip border is 18" wide with a 12" repeat.
Center, 24" x 24", features original, counted
cross stitch cowboys.

Joan Flynn. *Apple Basket.* Reversible quilt, 58 1/2" x 58 1/2" Three different three-strip strands are braided. Border is 9 3/4" wide with a 6 1/2" repeat. Center fabric was cut to fit.

The apple mosaic is the back of the quilt.

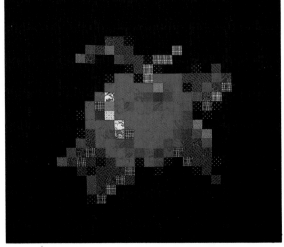

Planning Your Quilt

WATCH FOR THESE SYMBOLS
WHICH INDICATE A NEW STEP

PLANNING

ROTARY
CUTTING

MACHINE
SEWING

PRESSING

CHECK
POINT

SUPPLY CHECKLIST

- ☐ Rotary Cutter
- ☐ Cutting Mat
- ☐ Ruler with 1/8" markings
- ☐ 10" 45 Degree (Right Angle) Triangle or, 12" Quilter's Square
- ☐ 1/4" Grid Paper
- ☐ Tape

Selecting a Border

 The first step in making your Braided Border is to select a border, from the Tables on pages 33 through 39, that works with your center, or the center you plan to make.

If you plan to make the border first and then construct the center, your task is easy. Simply select a border width and decide on the number of strips per panel and you're ready to begin cutting. Several of the photos in the book show this border used very effectively around a single piece of fabric.

If you are putting the border around a block quilt, simply choose a repeat equal to the block size (or equal to 1/2 block, 1/3 block, 1/4 block). If your blocks are set on point, choose a repeat equal to the diagonal measurement of the block (or 1/2, 1/3 or 1/4 of the diagonal measurement).

Fitting a border to another existing center. Using the tables, find the width border you like and note the corresponding repeat. **Divide both the width and height of your center by the repeat — both answers must be whole numbers.** If dividing either width or height by your repeat results in a number with a fraction or decimal in the answer, you must look through the charts to find a repeat that does divide evenly into both the length and width of your center.

Example —

WIDTH OF BORDER — 3 3/4 inches
REPEAT OF BORDER — 2 1/2 inches

If your center is 30" x 40" and you have selected the 3 3/4" border width with a 2 1/2" repeat, divide each center dimension by the 2 1/2" repeat — 30 ÷ 2 1/2 = 12, 40 ÷ 2 1/2 = 16 — both answers are whole numbers so this border will fit your center.

There are cases where finding a perfect fit is not possible. If adding strips to float the center is not appropriate, the Braided Border may not be the right border choice.

After you select your border from the tables at the back of the book, fill in this chart for easy reference as you construct your border.

WIDTH OF BORDER _____
REPEAT OF BORDER _____

NUMBER OF STRIPS	WIDTH OF WIDE STRIPS	WIDTH OF WIDE PANEL	WIDTH OF NARROW STRIPS	WIDTH OF NARROW PANEL	LENGTH OF LONG SIDE OF TRIANGLE	INCHES OF BORDER PER YARD OF FABRIC

Sample Coloring Sheets

Coloring a few sample sheets can give you a good picture of how color and tone can work to create many different effects with this border. Coloring sheets for 2,3,4,5 and 6-strip borders are on pages 27-32. Make some copies and have some fun.

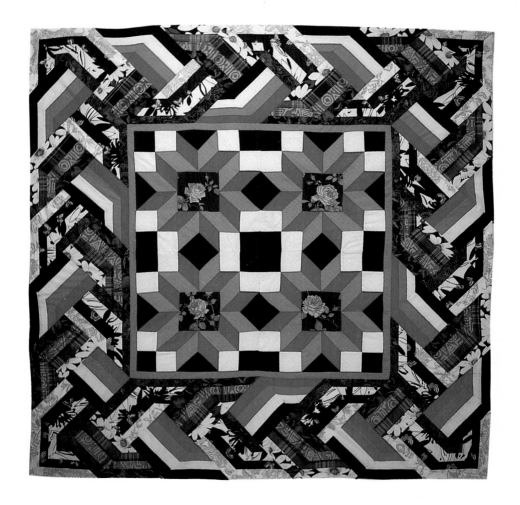

Judy Harris. *Let's Get Crazy*, 63" x 63"
Three different four-strip strands are braided.
Border is 13 1/2" wide with a 9" repeat. The center floats.

Tip: If you want to try braiding three different strands, plan carefully. It will work if your quilt is square, or if repeats on all sides are divisible by three.

Rotary Cutting

The rotary cutter is a very efficient tool for cutting fabric when properly used. The most common problem people have with their rotary cutters is trying to use the blades long after they are too dull to be safe. With a sharp rotary cutter, you should be able to cut your stack of fabric easily in one stroke. If you have a new blade and are still unable to cut your stack of fabric cleanly, you may have to cut fewer layers at a time. Rotary cutter safety is mostly common sense. If you are comfortable, in control, and can see what you are doing at all times, you should not have any trouble with the rotary cutter.

The cutting mat can also cause problems if it has scars from cutting too long in the same place — I have found that some boards "heal" better than others. A smooth mat is important to obtain clean cuts with no threads hanging on. Your ruler can affect your efficiency with the rotary cutter. It should be compatible with the rotary cutter — not metal, which damages blades, and not wood, which is easily cut. It should have a non-slip surface on the side that contacts the fabric.

THE BIG INCH

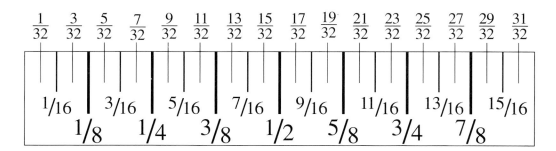

Use this giant inch to help locate the 1/32s on your ruler.

AN ACTUAL SIZE INCH

Making Your Border

Cutting Your Strips

Cut your strips the full width of the fabric. You can fold your fabric in half selvage-to-selvage to cut the strips, or cut across the full width with the fabric open. Choose the way which is most accurate for you. If you fold the fabric selvage-to-selvage, be careful to cut at 90 degrees to the fold so your strips will be straight. I fold my fabrics and stack them three high — so I am cutting through six layers. You may want to cut more or less; it doesn't matter as long as you are accurate.

The tables are figured in 1/32s of an inch and your ruler only goes to 1/8s. Use the Big Inch on the preceding page to help find the 1/32s on your ruler.

I suggest that you eyeball the 1/16s halfway between the 1/8s — the 1/32s are just a little bit more or less than the 1/16s. This seems pesky, and we're talking very small increments, but they can really add up — especially if you have chosen a border with 5 or 6 strips.

Set piles carefully aside and maintain fabric order.

John Flynn. 56" x 56"
This top is a variation of *King's X* with Barbara Johannah's
Governor's Palace Maze center. Four-strip border
is 12" wide with an 8" repeat. Fits 32" x 32" center.

Joan Flynn. *Braided Tile.* 54" x 54"
An original variation of the border. —
13 1/2" wide with a 9" repeat.

Joan Flynn. *Leftovers.*
You will have several inside triangle
pieces left after piecing a border.
Here are two ways of putting
them together.

Marking Your Sewing Machine

After eight years of quilting, I still like to mark the seam allowance on my machine with tape. **You will need to mark a 1/4" seam allowance.** To position the tape, first cut a 1 inch wide strip of 1/4 inch grid paper and sew along the right edge on the first 1/4 inch line for about one inch — the edge will mark the 1/4" seam allowance. Leave the paper in the machine while you position the tape on the machine.

I use masking tape. Some people prefer using a thicker tape or Moleskin™ so the fabric can ride right against the tape.

Many quilters use the edge of the presser foot as a guide. This is fine if it is an accurate 1/4" and you can maintain accuracy.

There are other methods of marking your machine such as a magnetic seam gauge (don't use on computerized machines) and a seam gauge made to screw onto the machine deck.

Whatever method you choose, take the time to check the accuracy. I have seen some pretty erratic results and the Braided Border is not a forgiving pattern when it comes to seam allowance.

You are ready to begin sewing your strips together.

Sewing the Strips Together

Organize your strips so you can sew your panels easily without getting the order of the strips mixed up. If you cut with the strips folded, it's easiest if you put all of each color in separate piles and put the piles in order. If you stacked all your fabrics open and in order and cut through the entire stack at once, you're ready to sew each stack into a panel. Organize both your narrow and wide strips in one of these ways.

Checking the Width of Your Strips

To check your seam allowance as you go, sew two strips together and press the seam to one side. **The width of the pair of strips should be two times the strip width minus 1/2". This must be accurate.** If the measurement is off, check the marking on your machine. You must adjust your seam allowance until the measurement is accurate.

Sewing Tip:
I start two strips into the machine and then insert my index finger between the two strips, holding equal tension on the top fabric (thumb and index finger) and bottom fabric (middle and index fingers). By manipulating my thumb and middle finger, I can keep the fabric lined up while sewing continuously instead of having to stop to realign the strips along the way.

This may take a little practice to master, but your sewing will go more smoothly.

Pressing the Strips

I press the strips after each seam, as I go. I find it is easier to sew this way and, even if it is a little harder to press without distortion, I think it is worth it.

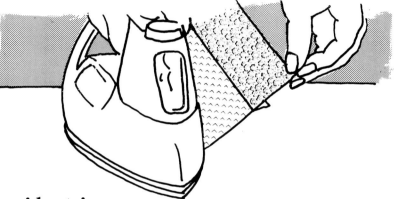

Tip:
It is best to press on the right side of the fabric.

Press the seams in your wide strips the opposite direction of those in your narrow strips.

PRESS SEAMS
IN OPPOSITE
DIRECTIONS

WIDE $\longrightarrow$ $\longleftarrow$ NARROW

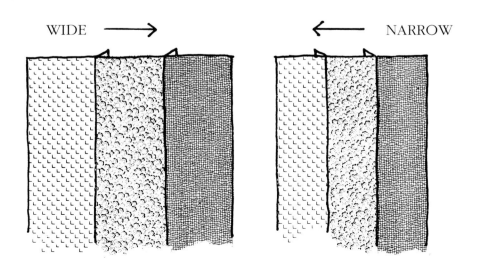

Cutting the Panels

The Wide Panels. First, check the width of the wide panels.
They must be within 1/16" of the "Width of Wide Panel"
measurement given in the Table.
If width is off, resew before cutting.

True up the ends
of the panels as
needed. Line up one
of the lines on your ruler
on a seam to establish the
90° angle for squaring your
panels.

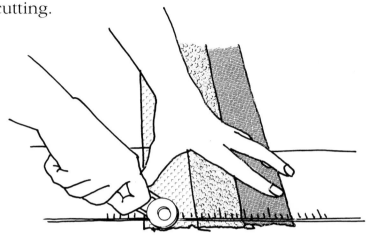

Cut the wide panels so the length
is the same as the "Width of Wide Panel"
measurement given in the Table.
Be sure to make your cuts square
(90 degrees) to the seams in the panel.

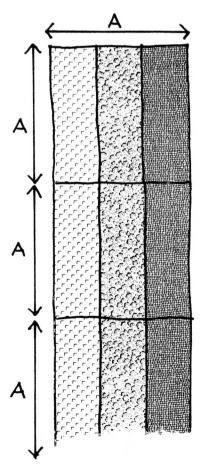

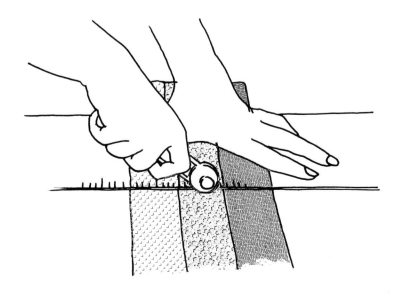

The Narrow Panels.
Check your panel width
as you did for the wide panels.

Next, cut the end off of the panel
on a 45 degree angle with the
outside triangle fabric in position
as shown. Place the long side of the
triangle on a seam, and lay your
ruler against the triangle to
establish the angle of the cut.
Remove the triangle and
use the ruler to cut
the end of the panel.

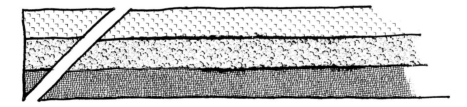

Refer to your Table for the "Length of Long Side of Triangle" measurement.
Mark on the outside triangle fabric and line up the triangle along the
cut end and the mark, as shown.

Take a minute while you have the triangle
in position to mark both sides with tape
so you won't have to measure each time.

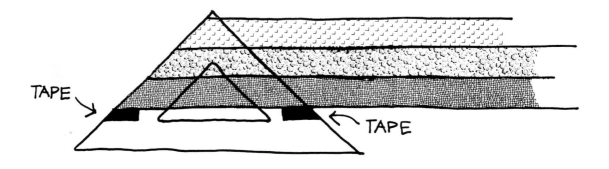

TAPE

TAPE

Cut the first outside triangle.

There should be a flat spot
1/4" wide at the top
of the triangle.

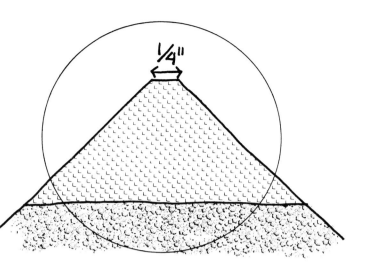

Continue to cut inside and outside triangles,
alternating from side to side, from the narrow strips.
To border a standard, square-cornered quilt, you will need 12 more
outside triangles than inside triangles. (You'll find a use for the extra
triangles, I'm sure. There doesn't seem to be any practical way of
eliminating them. See "Leftovers," page 15.) If you are cutting the corners,
as I did on "King's X," you can eliminate two outside triangles per corner.

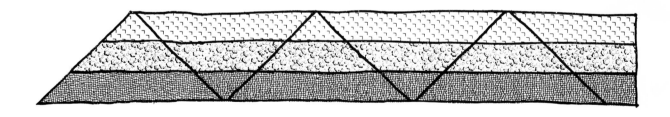

OUTSIDE
TRIANGLES

INSIDE
TRIANGLES

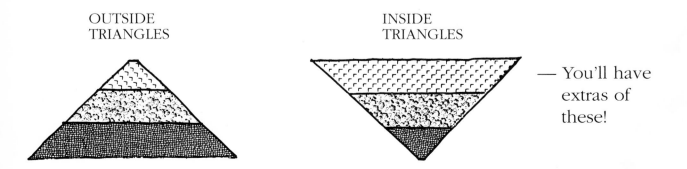

— You'll have
extras of
these!

Piecing the Border

Now you must decide which way you want your braid to go — clockwise or counterclockwise. It doesn't look a lot different either way, but you must remain consistent throughout your project or the braid won't be continuous. Lay out a few repeats of the braid so you can get the pattern.

These are the basic units —

OUTSIDE TRIANGLE/SQUARE UNITS   INSIDE TRIANGLE/SQUARE UNITS

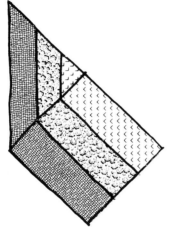 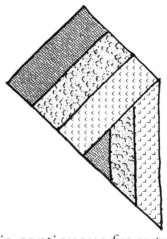

Carefully match the seams where the braid is continuous from triangle to square. All seams should be sewn as accurately as possible because there are so many seams and even small errors will accumulate and distort the final size of your border.

Border Units.

The Border Unit is made up of one of each of the units above.

If you have a repeat of 5 or more, sew three border units together and check your repeat length with the figure in your Table. If the repeat is correct, proceed to sew the units together.

Getting Around the Corner

Now is a good time to get out the coloring sheet you did for your quilt and plan how to sew your border together. We show two methods here.

I put my border units together in long strings with the corners built on the end so that the quilt is set into the border corner. Some people find it easier to build the corner separately and sew it on last to avoid the set-in corner. Each method has its advantages. I like setting in the quilt because it is easier to keep track of the braid when I build the whole side together. On a quilt like Peggy's "Ride 'em Cowboy," page 6, the corners are actually the biggest area of the quilt and the other method works better — and she did avoid the set-in corners!

The Governor's Palace Maze Design
by Barbara Johannah

The design of my *King's X* quilt is a combination of Barbara Johannah's intriguing *Governor's Palace Maze* center and my rainbow Braided Border. Follow these easy instructions to make your own quilt.

First, color the planning page. The design is most efficient if you balance the number of pairs of triangles — use the same number of triangles 1 and 2 for each color pair.

Calculate the strip width. (On King's X, the small squares are 6" x 6". The strip width is $(6 \times 1.41) \div 4 + 1/2 = 2.62$, or 2 5/8". The long side of the triangle equals $6 \times 1.41 + 1.25 = 9.71$, or 9 3/4".)

Refer to the Table below for other square sizes.

SQUARE SIZE	STRIP WIDTH	LONG SIDE OF TRIANGLE	BRAID REPEAT
3"	1 9/16"	5 1/2"	6"
4"	1 15/16"	6 7/8"	8"
5"	2 1/4"	8 5/16"	10"
6"	2 5/8"	9 3/4"	12"

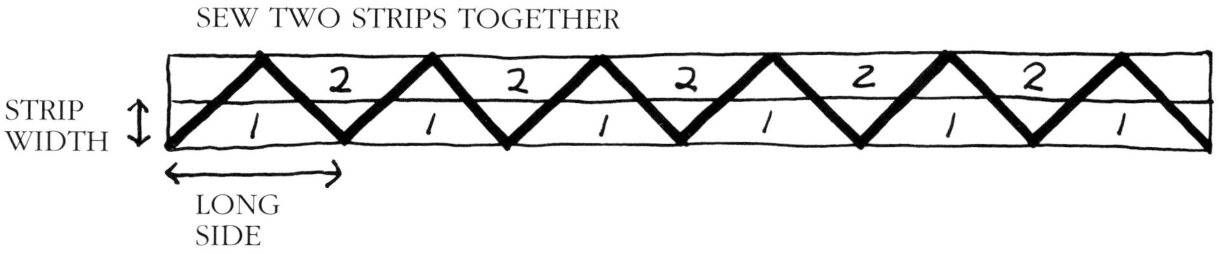

SEW TWO STRIPS TOGETHER

STRIP WIDTH

LONG SIDE

Finishing Your Quilt

I suggest quilting in the ditch on the Braided Border.
This defines and emphasizes the strands of the braid.
If your border has a wide strip width, additional
quilting down the center of each strip
might be a nice addition.

On the *King's X* center, I quilted
around each color segment.

DO NOT
QUILT
ON THIS
SEAM —
IT WOULD
DISRUPT
THE BRAID.

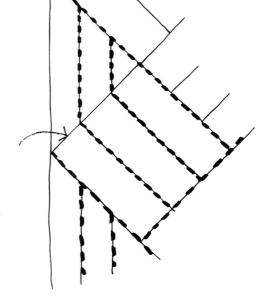

I hand quilt on a Flynn Quilt Frame,
but this pattern can be quilted
very effectively on the machine.

BRAIDED BORDER *Coloring Sheet*
2 STRIP

BRAIDED BORDER *Coloring Sheet*
3 STRIP

BRAIDED BORDER *Coloring Sheet*
4 STRIP

BRAIDED BORDER *Coloring Sheet*
6 STRIP

BRAIDED BORDER *Coloring Sheet*

3 STRIP

5 STRIP

32

Braided Border Planning Charts

Planning Charts are included for borders ranging from 3 3/4" to 18" in width. The charts include measurements for braids made of 2, 3, 4, 5 and 6 strips through the 9" width. Charts for wider borders — 9 3/4" and up — give measurements using 3, 4, 5 and 6 strips. The two-strip border is most successful on the narrower sizes.

If you want to make a border with a width and repeat which falls between the measurements on the charts, you can just split the difference in half. If you do this, I suggest that you make a test square and a triangle and sew them together to check your measurements.

WIDTH OF BORDER — 3 3/4 inches
REPEAT OF BORDER — 2 1/2 inches

NUMBER OF STRIPS	WIDTH OF WIDE STRIPS	WIDTH OF WIDE PANEL	WIDTH OF NARROW STRIPS	WIDTH OF NARROW PANEL	LENGTH OF LONG SIDE OF TRIANGLE	INCHES OF BORDER PER YARD OF FABRIC
2	1-3/8"	2-1/4"	1-1/8"	1-3/4"	3-3/4"	307"
3	1-3/32"	2-1/4"	29/32"	1-3/4"	3-3/4"	377"
4	15/16"	2-1/4"	13/16"	1-3/4"	3-3/4"	426"
5	27/32"	2-1/4"	3/4"	1-3/4"	3-3/4"	461"
6	13/16"	2-1/4"	23/32"	1-3/4"	3-3/4"	488"

WIDTH OF BORDER — 4 1/2 inches
REPEAT OF BORDER — 3 inches

NUMBER OF STRIPS	WIDTH OF WIDE STRIPS	WIDTH OF WIDE PANEL	WIDTH OF NARROW STRIPS	WIDTH OF NARROW PANEL	LENGTH OF LONG SIDE OF TRIANGLE	INCHES OF BORDER PER YARD OF FABRIC
2	1-9/16"	2-5/8"	1-1/4"	2"	4-1/4"	287"
3	1-7/32"	2-5/8"	1"	2"	4-1/4"	359"
4	1-1/32"	2-5/8"	7/8"	2"	4-1/4"	410"
5	15/16"	2-5/8"	13/16"	2"	4-1/4"	449"
6	27/32"	2-5/8"	3/4"	2"	4-1/4"	479"

WIDTH OF BORDER — 5 1/4 inches
REPEAT OF BORDER — 3 1/2 inches

NUMBER OF STRIPS	WIDTH OF WIDE STRIPS	WIDTH OF WIDE PANEL	WIDTH OF NARROW STRIPS	WIDTH OF NARROW PANEL	LENGTH OF LONG SIDE OF TRIANGLE	INCHES OF BORDER PER YARD OF FABRIC
2	1-3/4"	3"	1-3/8"	2-1/4"	4-3/4"	268"
3	1-3/8"	3"	1-3/32"	2-1/4"	4-3/4"	341"
4	1-1/8"	3"	15/16"	2-1/4"	4-3/4"	394"
5	1"	3"	27/32"	2-1/4"	4-3/4"	434"
6	29/32"	3"	13/16"	2-1/4"	4-3/4"	466"

WIDTH OF BORDER — 6 inches
REPEAT OF BORDER — 4 inches

NUMBER OF STRIPS	WIDTH OF WIDE STRIPS	WIDTH OF WIDE PANEL	WIDTH OF NARROW STRIPS	WIDTH OF NARROW PANEL	LENGTH OF LONG SIDE OF TRIANGLE	INCHES OF BORDER PER YARD OF FABRIC
2	1-29/32"	3-5/16"	1-1/2"	2-1/2"	5-1/4"	251"
3	1-7/16"	3-5/16"	1-5/32"	2-1/2"	5-1/4"	323"
4	1-7/32"	3-5/16"	1"	2-1/2"	5-1/4"	377"
5	1-1/16"	3-5/16"	29/32"	2-1/2"	5-1/4"	419"
6	31/32"	3-5/16"	27/32"	2-1/2"	5-1/4"	452"

WIDTH OF BORDER — 6 3/4 inches
REPEAT OF BORDER — 4 1/2 inches

NUMBER OF STRIPS	WIDTH OF WIDE STRIPS	WIDTH OF WIDE PANEL	WIDTH OF NARROW STRIPS	WIDTH OF NARROW PANEL	LENGTH OF LONG SIDE OF TRIANGLE	INCHES OF BORDER PER YARD OF FABRIC
2	2-3/32"	3-11/16"	1-5/8"	2-3/4"	5-3/4"	236"
3	1-9/16"	3-11/16"	1-1/4"	2-3/4"	5-3/4"	307"
4	1-9/32"	3-11/16"	1-1/16"	2-3/4"	5-3/4"	361"
5	1-1/8"	3-11/16"	15/16"	2-3/4"	5-3/4"	404"
6	1-1/32"	3-11/16"	7/8"	2-3/4"	5-3/4"	438"

WIDTH OF BORDER — 7 1/2 inches
REPEAT OF BORDER — 5 inches

NUMBER OF STRIPS	WIDTH OF WIDE STRIPS	WIDTH OF WIDE PANEL	WIDTH OF NARROW STRIPS	WIDTH OF NARROW PANEL	LENGTH OF LONG SIDE OF TRIANGLE	INCHES OF BORDER PER YARD OF FABRIC
2	2-1/4"	4-1/32"	1-3/4"	3"	6-1/4"	222"
3	1-11/16"	4-1/32"	1-11/32"	3"	6-1/4"	292"
4	1-3/8"	4-1/32"	1-1/8"	3"	6-1/4"	345"
5	1-7/32"	4-1/32"	1"	3"	6-1/4"	389"
6	1-3/32"	4-1/32"	29/32"	3"	6-1/4"	424"

WIDTH OF BORDER — 8 1/4 inches
REPEAT OF BORDER — 5 1/2 inches

NUMBER OF STRIPS	WIDTH OF WIDE STRIPS	WIDTH OF WIDE PANEL	WIDTH OF NARROW STRIPS	WIDTH OF NARROW PANEL	LENGTH OF LONG SIDE OF TRIANGLE	INCHES OF BORDER PER YARD OF FABRIC
2	2-7/16"	4-3/8"	1-7/8"	3-1/4"	6-3/4"	210"
3	1-13/16"	4-3/8"	1-13/32"	3-1/4"	6-3/4"	277"
4	1-15/32"	4-3/8"	1-3/16"	3-1/4"	6-3/4"	331"
5	1-9/32"	4-3/8"	1-1/16"	3-1/4"	6-3/4"	374"
6	1-5/32"	4-3/8"	31/32"	3-1/4"	6-3/4"	410"

WIDTH OF BORDER — 9 inches
REPEAT OF BORDER — 6 inches

NUMBER OF STRIPS	WIDTH OF WIDE STRIPS	WIDTH OF WIDE PANEL	WIDTH OF NARROW STRIPS	WIDTH OF NARROW PANEL	LENGTH OF LONG SIDE OF TRIANGLE	INCHES OF BORDER PER YARD OF FABRIC
2	2-5/8"	4-3/4"	2"	3-1/2"	7-1/4"	198"
3	1-29/32"	4-3/4"	1-1/2"	3-1/2"	7-1/4"	265"
4	1-9/16"	4-3/4"	1-1/4"	3-1/2"	7-1/4"	317"
5	1-11/32"	4-3/4"	1-3/32"	3-1/2"	7-1/4"	361"
6	1-7/32"	4-3/4"	1"	3-1/2"	7-1/4"	397"

WIDTH OF BORDER — 9 3/4 inches
REPEAT OF BORDER — 6 1/2 inches

NUMBER OF STRIPS	WIDTH OF WIDE STRIPS	WIDTH OF WIDE PANEL	WIDTH OF NARROW STRIPS	WIDTH OF NARROW PANEL	LENGTH OF LONG SIDE OF TRIANGLE	INCHES OF BORDER PER YARD OF FABRIC
3	2-1/32"	5-3/32"	1-19/32"	3-3/4"	7-3/4"	253"
4	1-21/32"	5-3/32"	1-5/16"	3-3/4"	7-3/4"	305"
5	1-13/32"	5-3/32"	1-5/32"	3-3/4"	7-3/4"	348"
6	1-1/4"	5-3/32"	1-1/32"	3-3/4"	7-3/4"	384"

WIDTH OF BORDER — 10 1/2 inches
REPEAT OF BORDER — 7 inches

NUMBER OF STRIPS	WIDTH OF WIDE STRIPS	WIDTH OF WIDE PANEL	WIDTH OF NARROW STRIPS	WIDTH OF NARROW PANEL	LENGTH OF LONG SIDE OF TRIANGLE	INCHES OF BORDER PER YARD OF FABRIC
3	2-5/32"	5-7/16"	1-21/32"	4"	8-1/4"	242"
4	1-3/4"	5-7/16"	1-3/8"	4"	8-1/4"	293"
5	1-1/2"	5-7/16"	1-3/16"	4"	8-1/4"	336"
6	1-3/8"	5-7/16"	1-3/32"	4"	8-1/4"	372"

WIDTH OF BORDER — 11 1/4 inches
REPEAT OF BORDER — 7 1/2 inches

NUMBER OF STRIPS	WIDTH OF WIDE STRIPS	WIDTH OF WIDE PANEL	WIDTH OF NARROW STRIPS	WIDTH OF NARROW PANEL	LENGTH OF LONG SIDE OF TRIANGLE	INCHES OF BORDER PER YARD OF FABRIC
3	2-1/4"	5-13/16"	1-3/4"	4-1/4"	8-3/4"	232"
4	1-13/16"	5-13/16"	1-7/16"	4-1/4"	8-3/4"	282"
5	1-9/16"	5-13/16"	1-1/4"	4-1/4"	8-3/4"	324"
6	1-3/8"	5-13/16"	1-1/8"	4-1/4"	8-3/4"	360"

WIDTH OF BORDER — 12 inches
REPEAT OF BORDER — 8 inches

NUMBER OF STRIPS	WIDTH OF WIDE STRIPS	WIDTH OF WIDE PANEL	WIDTH OF NARROW STRIPS	WIDTH OF NARROW PANEL	LENGTH OF LONG SIDE OF TRIANGLE	INCHES OF BORDER PER YARD OF FABRIC
3	2-3/8"	6-5/32"	1-27/32"	4-1/2"	9-1/4"	222"
4	1-29/32"	6-5/32"	1-1/2"	4-1/2"	9-1/4"	272"
5	1-5/8"	6-5/32"	1-11/32"	4-1/2"	9-1/4"	314"
6	1-7/16"	6-5/32"	1-5/32"	4-1/2"	9-1/4"	349"

WIDTH OF BORDER — 12 3/4 inches
REPEAT OF BORDER — 8 1/2 inches

NUMBER OF STRIPS	WIDTH OF WIDE STRIPS	WIDTH OF WIDE PANEL	WIDTH OF NARROW STRIPS	WIDTH OF NARROW PANEL	LENGTH OF LONG SIDE OF TRIANGLE	INCHES OF BORDER PER YARD OF FABRIC
3	2-1/2"	6-1/2"	1-29/32"	4-3/4"	9-3/4"	214"
4	2"	6-1/2"	1-9/16"	4-3/4"	9-3/4"	262"
5	1-23/32"	6-1/2"	1-11/32"	4-3/4"	9-3/4"	303"
6	1-1/2"	6-1/2"	1-7/32"	4-3/4"	9-3/4"	339"

WIDTH OF BORDER — 13 1/2 inches
REPEAT OF BORDER — 9 inches

NUMBER OF STRIPS	WIDTH OF WIDE STRIPS	WIDTH OF WIDE PANEL	WIDTH OF NARROW STRIPS	WIDTH OF NARROW PANEL	LENGTH OF LONG SIDE OF TRIANGLE	INCHES OF BORDER PER YARD OF FABRIC
3	2-5/8"	6-7/8"	2"	5"	10-1/4"	206"
4	2-3/32"	6-7/8"	1-5/8"	5"	10-1/4"	253"
5	1-25/32"	6-7/8"	1-13/32"	5"	10-1/4"	294"
6	1-9/16"	6-7/8"	1-1/4"	5"	10-1/4"	329"

WIDTH OF BORDER — 14 1/4 inches
REPEAT OF BORDER — 9 1/2 inches

NUMBER OF STRIPS	WIDTH OF WIDE STRIPS	WIDTH OF WIDE PANEL	WIDTH OF NARROW STRIPS	WIDTH OF NARROW PANEL	LENGTH OF LONG SIDE OF TRIANGLE	INCHES OF BORDER PER YARD OF FABRIC
3	2-3/4"	7-7/32"	2-3/32"	5-1/4"	10-3/4"	198"
4	2-5/32"	7-7/32"	1-11/16"	5-1/4"	10-3/4"	245"
5	1-27/32"	7-7/32"	1-7/16"	5-1/4"	10-3/4"	285"
6	1-5/8"	7-7/32"	1-9/32"	5-1/4"	10-3/4"	320"

WIDTH OF BORDER — 15 inches
REPEAT OF BORDER — 10 inches

NUMBER OF STRIPS	WIDTH OF WIDE STRIPS	WIDTH OF WIDE PANEL	WIDTH OF NARROW STRIPS	WIDTH OF NARROW PANEL	LENGTH OF LONG SIDE OF TRIANGLE	INCHES OF BORDER PER YARD OF FABRIC
3	2-27/32"	7-9/16"	2-5/32"	5-1/2"	11-1/4"	191"
4	2-1/4"	7-9/16"	1-3/4"	5-1/2"	11-1/4"	237"
5	1-29/32"	7-9/16"	1-1/2"	5-1/2"	11-1/4"	276"
6	1-11/16"	7-9/16"	1-5/16"	5-1/2"	11- 1/4"	311"

WIDTH OF BORDER — 15 3/4 inches
REPEAT OF BORDER —10 1/2 inches

NUMBER OF STRIPS	WIDTH OF WIDE STRIPS	WIDTH OF WIDE PANEL	WIDTH OF NARROW STRIPS	WIDTH OF NARROW PANEL	LENGTH OF LONG SIDE OF TRIANGLE	INCHES OF BORDER PER YARD OF FABRIC
3	3"	7-15/16"	2-1/4"	5-3/4"	11-3/4"	185"
4	2-11/32"	7-15/16"	1-13/16"	5-3/4"	11-3/4"	229"
5	2"	7-15/16"	1-9/16"	5-3/4"	11-3/4"	268"
6	1-3/4"	7-15/16"	1-3/8"	5-3/4"	11-3/4"	302"

WIDTH OF BORDER — 16 1/2 inches
REPEAT OF BORDER — 11 inches

NUMBER OF STRIPS	WIDTH OF WIDE STRIPS	WIDTH OF WIDE PANEL	WIDTH OF NARROW STRIPS	WIDTH OF NARROW PANEL	LENGTH OF LONG SIDE OF TRIANGLE	INCHES OF BORDER PER YARD OF FABRIC
3	3-3/32"	8-9/32"	2-11/32"	6"	12-1/4"	179"
4	2-7/16"	8-9/32"	1-7/8"	6"	12-1/4"	222"
5	2-1/16"	8-9/32"	1-19/32"	6"	12-1/4"	261"
6	1-13/16"	8-9/32"	1-13/32"	6"	12-1/4"	294"

WIDTH OF BORDER — 17 1/4 inches
REPEAT OF BORDER — 11 1/2 inches

NUMBER OF STRIPS	WIDTH OF WIDE STRIPS	WIDTH OF WIDE PANEL	WIDTH OF NARROW STRIPS	WIDTH OF NARROW PANEL	LENGTH OF LONG SIDE OF TRIANGLE	INCHES OF BORDER PER YARD OF FABRIC
3	3-7/32"	8-5/8"	2-13/32"	6-1/4"	12-3/4"	173"
4	2-17/32"	8-5/8"	1-15/16"	6-1/4"	12-3/4"	216"
5	2-1/8"	8-5/8"	1-25/32"	6-1/4"	12-3/4"	253"
6	1-27/32"	8-5/8"	1-15/32"	6-1/4"	12-3/4"	287"

WIDTH OF BORDER — 18 inches
REPEAT OF BORDER — 12 inches

NUMBER OF STRIPS	WIDTH OF WIDE STRIPS	WIDTH OF WIDE PANEL	WIDTH OF NARROW STRIPS	WIDTH OF NARROW PANEL	LENGTH OF LONG SIDE OF TRIANGLE	INCHES OF BORDER PER YARD OF FABRIC
3	3-11/32"	9"	2-1/2"	6-1/2"	13-1/4"	167"
4	2-5/8"	9"	2"	6-1/2"	13-1/4"	209"
5	2-3/16"	9"	1-11/16"	6-1/2"	13-1/4"	246"
6	1-29/32"	9"	1-1/2"	6-1/2"	13-1/4"	279"